THE WORLD'S WORST NATURAL

# THE WORLD'S WORST TORNADOES

by John R. Baker

CAPSTONE PRESS
a capstone imprint

Blazers Books are published by Capstone Press,
1710 Roe Crest Drive, North Mankato, Minnesota 56003
www.mycapstone.com

Copyright © 2017 by Capstone Press, a Capstone imprint. All rights reserved. No part of this publication may be reproduced in whole or in part, or stored in a retrieval system, or transmitted in any form or by any means, electronic, mechanical, photocopying, recording, or otherwise, without written permission of the publisher.

**Library of Congress Cataloging-in-Publication Data**
Names: Baker, John R. (John Ronald), 1989–
Title: The world's worst tornadoes / by John R. Baker.
Description: North Mankato, Minnesota: Capstone Press, 2017. | Series: Blazers. World's worst natural disasters | Audience: Grades 4 to 6. | Includes bibliographical references and index. | Description based on print version record and CIP data provided by publisher; resource not viewed.
Identifiers: LCCN 2016000445 (print) | LCCN 2015049414 (ebook) | ISBN 9781515717966 (eBook PDF) | ISBN 9781515717881 (library binding) | ISBN 9781515717928 (paperback)
Subjects: LCSH: Tornadoes—History—Juvenile literature.
Classification: LCC QC955.2 (print) | LCC QC955.2 .B34 2017 (ebook) | DDC 551.55/309—dc23
LC record available at http://lccn.loc.gov/2016000445

Summary: Describes history's biggest and most destructive tornadoes from around the world.

**Editorial Credits**
Aaron Sautter, editor; Steve Mead, designer; Jo Miller, media researcher; Tori Abraham, production specialist

**Photo Credits**
AP Images, 18–19, Pavel Rahman, 12–13; Getty Images: AFP Photo/Ross Tuckerman, 22–23, Hulton Archive/Topical Press Agency, 6–7, Jerry Laizure, 8–9, Jordan Mansfield, 16–17, Zachary Roberts, 20–21; Newscom: EPA/Ken Blackbird, 24–25, UPI/Tom Uhlenbrock, 14–15, ZUMA Press/Ken Stewart, 10–11, ZUMA Press/St Petersburg Times, 28–29; Shutterstock: EmiliaUngur, 4–5, leonello calvetti, cover, 3, 31, Martin Hass, cover, Minerva Studio, 26–27

**Design Elements**
Shutterstock: solarseven, xpixel

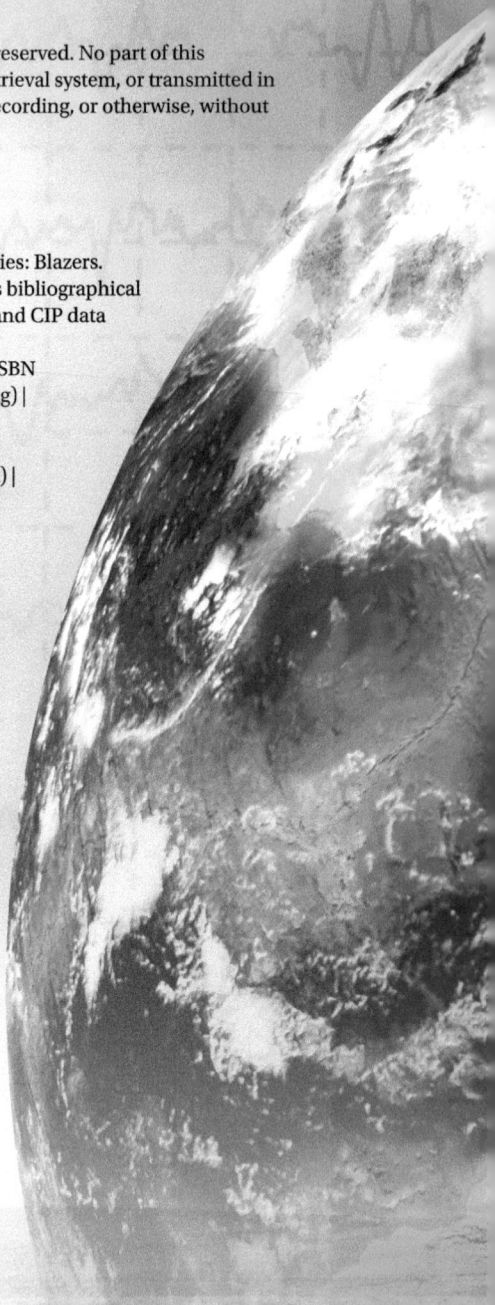

Printed in the United States 5702

# TABLE OF CONTENTS

**Nature's Power Unleashed** ..... **4**
**Tri-State Terror** ..... **6**
**Monster in Oklahoma** ..... **8**
**1974 Super Outbreak** ..... **10**
**Disaster in Bangladesh** ..... **12**
**A Direct Hit** ..... **14**
**British Outbreak** ..... **16**
**Topeka Twister** ..... **18**
**Canadian Cyclone** ..... **20**
**One Powerful Storm** ..... **22**
**A Supersized Monster** ..... **24**
**A Tornado Factory** ..... **26**
**Tornado Safety** ..... **28**

Glossary ..... 30
Read More ..... 31
Internet Sites ..... 31
Critical Thinking Using the Common Core ..... 32
Index ..... 32

# NATURE'S POWER UNLEASHED

The Enhanced Fujita (EF) Scale measures a tornado's strength. An EF0 tornado is the weakest. It does the least amount of damage. An EF5 tornado is the most powerful. It causes the most destruction.

Trees snapped in half. Roofs ripped off buildings. Cars tossed around like toys. What did this? A tornado! These powerful twisting storms cause damage around the world every year. Hang on tight. It's time to learn about the world's worst tornadoes.

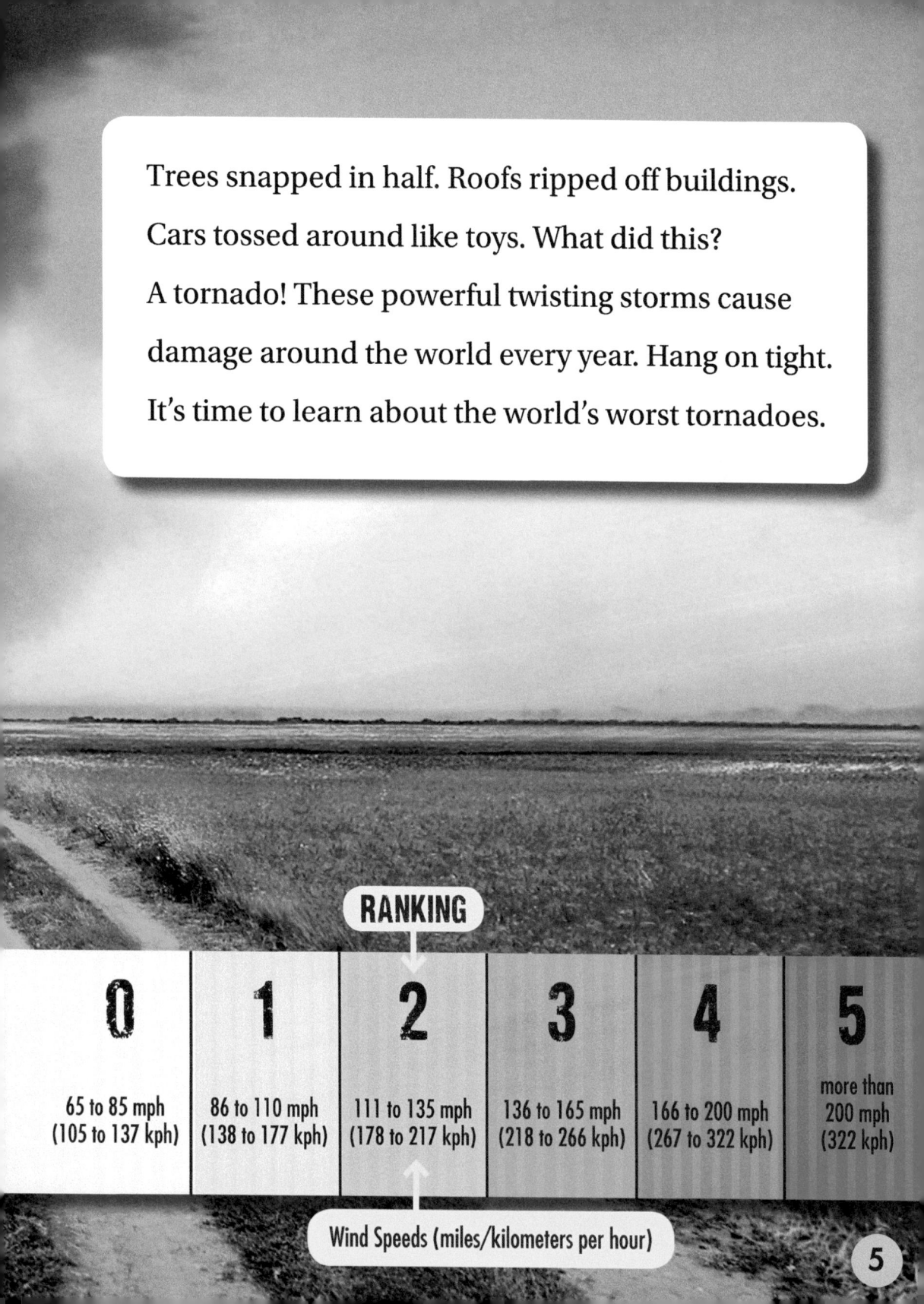

# TRI-STATE TERROR

**Location:**
Missouri, Illinois, Indiana

**Date:**
March 18, 1925

**EF Rating:**

5
4
3
2
1
0

On March 18, 1925, one tornado set a record. The monster twister stayed on the ground for an incredible 219 miles (352 km)! It destroyed entire towns across three states. The Tri-State Tornado was the deadliest in U.S. history. It killed 695 people.

**FACT**

Tornadoes are often known by other names such as twisters or **cyclones**.

**cyclone**—a fast spinning column of air

# MONSTER IN OKLAHOMA

**Location:**
Oklahoma City, Oklahoma

**Date:**
May 3, 1999

**EF Rating:**

May 3, 1999, was a dark day in Oklahoma City. A giant, 1-mile- (1.6-km-) wide tornado destroyed entire neighborhoods. Streets were filled with broken trees and shattered homes. The giant twister caused more than $1 billion of damage. It killed 36 people.

**FACT**

The Oklahoma City tornado had wind speeds up to 318 miles (512 km) per hour. It was the fastest tornado wind speed ever recorded.

# 1974 SUPER OUTBREAK

**Location:**
Midwest and eastern United States

**Date:**
April 3–4, 1974

**EF Rating:**

Huge storms swept across North America on April 3 and 4, 1974. They created a record **outbreak** of more than 140 tornadoes. The twisters caused death and destruction in 13 U.S. states and Canada. At least 65 of those twisters were rated EF3 or higher.

**FACT**

The 1974 Super Outbreak killed more than 300 people. The twisters also caused more than $600 million in damage.

**outbreak**—a large number of events that occur in a certain area

# DISASTER IN BANGLADESH

**Location:**
Dhaka, Bangladesh

**Date:**
April 26, 1989

**EF Rating:**
unknown

The world's deadliest tornado occurred on April 26, 1989. The killer twister hit near Dhaka, Bangladesh. About 1,300 people died as it tore through thousands of homes. Another 12,000 suffered injuries in the storm.

**FACT**

The deadly storm in Bangladesh left 80,000 people without homes.

# A DIRECT HIT

**Location:**
Joplin, Missouri

**Date:**
May 22, 2011

**EF Rating:**

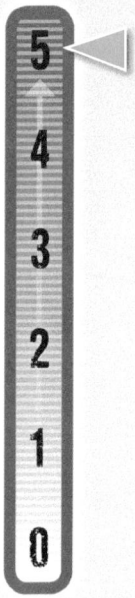

A nightmare visited Joplin, Missouri, on May 22, 2011. A giant EF5 twister plowed a path of destruction through the middle of the town. It killed more than 150 people. It also did $2.8 billion in damage. It was the costliest tornado in history.

**FACT**

In April 2011, more than 750 tornadoes were recorded in the United States, setting a new record.

# BRITISH OUTBREAK

**Location:**
Great Britain

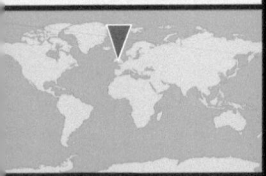

**Date:**
November 23, 1981

**EF Rating:**

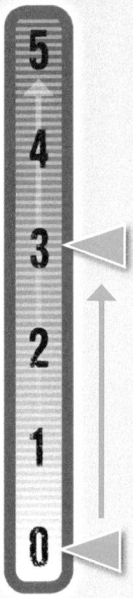


No place in the world is safe from tornadoes. On November 23, 1981, a record 105 twisters hit Great Britain. The county of Norfolk saw at least 13 tornadoes touch down. Most of them were weak and didn't last long.

**FACT**

Tornadoes in the United Kingdom are rated using the International Tornado Intensity Scale. The weakest storms have a T0 rating. The strongest are rated T11.

# TOPEKA TWISTER

**Location:**
Topeka, Kansas

**Date:**
June 8, 1966

**EF Rating:**

5
4
3
2
1
0

It was a **humid** summer day on June 8, 1966. That evening a giant EF5 tornado headed straight for Topeka, Kansas. It tore a 22-mile-(35-km-) long path through the city. The fierce storm damaged 3,000 homes. It killed 16 people. Another 500 were injured.

**FACT**

The tornado in Topeka caused $250 million in damage. Today that price would be more than $1.6 billion. It was one of the costliest twisters in U.S. history.

**humid**—damp and moist

# CANADIAN CYCLONE

**Location:**
Regina, Saskatchewan, Canada

**Date:**
June 30, 1912

**EF Rating:**

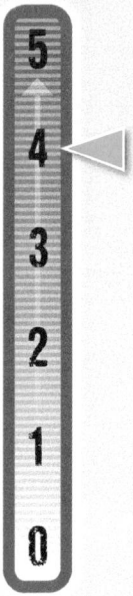

In 1912 Regina was a thriving city in Saskatchewan, Canada. On June 30 a tornado destroyed much of the city. The cyclone flattened homes. It reduced brick buildings to rubble. The twister left 2,500 people with no place to live.

**FACT**

The Regina twister killed 28 people. That's more than any other tornado in Canada's history.

# ONE POWERFUL STORM

**Location:**
Bucca, Australia

**Date:**
November 29, 1992

**EF Rating:**

Most tornadoes in Australia aren't very strong. But a powerful EF4 twister struck the small town of Bucca on November 29, 1992. It had wind speeds of 166 miles (267 km) per hour. The storm also carried baseball-sized **hail**. It was the strongest tornado ever seen in Australia.

**FACT**

On November 4, 1973, a tornado ripped up more than 1,300 buildings near Brisbane. It caused more damage than any other twister in Australia's history.

**hail**—balls of ice that fall during a thunderstorm

# A SUPERSIZED MONSTER

**Location:**
Hallam, Nebraska

**Date:**
May 22, 2004

**EF Rating:**

5
4
3
2
1
0

The widest twister ever recorded hit Hallam, Nebraska, in 2004. This supersized EF5 monster stretched 2.5 miles (4 km) wide. Mud and **debris** from the small town's buildings filled the streets.

**FACT**

The Hallam tornado destroyed 150 homes. It also wiped out the town's schools, post office, churches, and office buildings.

**debris**—the scattered pieces of something that has been broken or destroyed

# A TORNADO FACTORY

**Location:**
southeastern United States

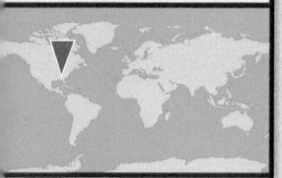

**Date:**
September 15–18, 2004

**EF Rating:**

**Hurricanes** often form dozens of tornadoes. In 2004 Hurricane Ivan set a record for the most twisters created by a hurricane. When Ivan hit the southeastern United States, it formed 117 tornadoes over four days.

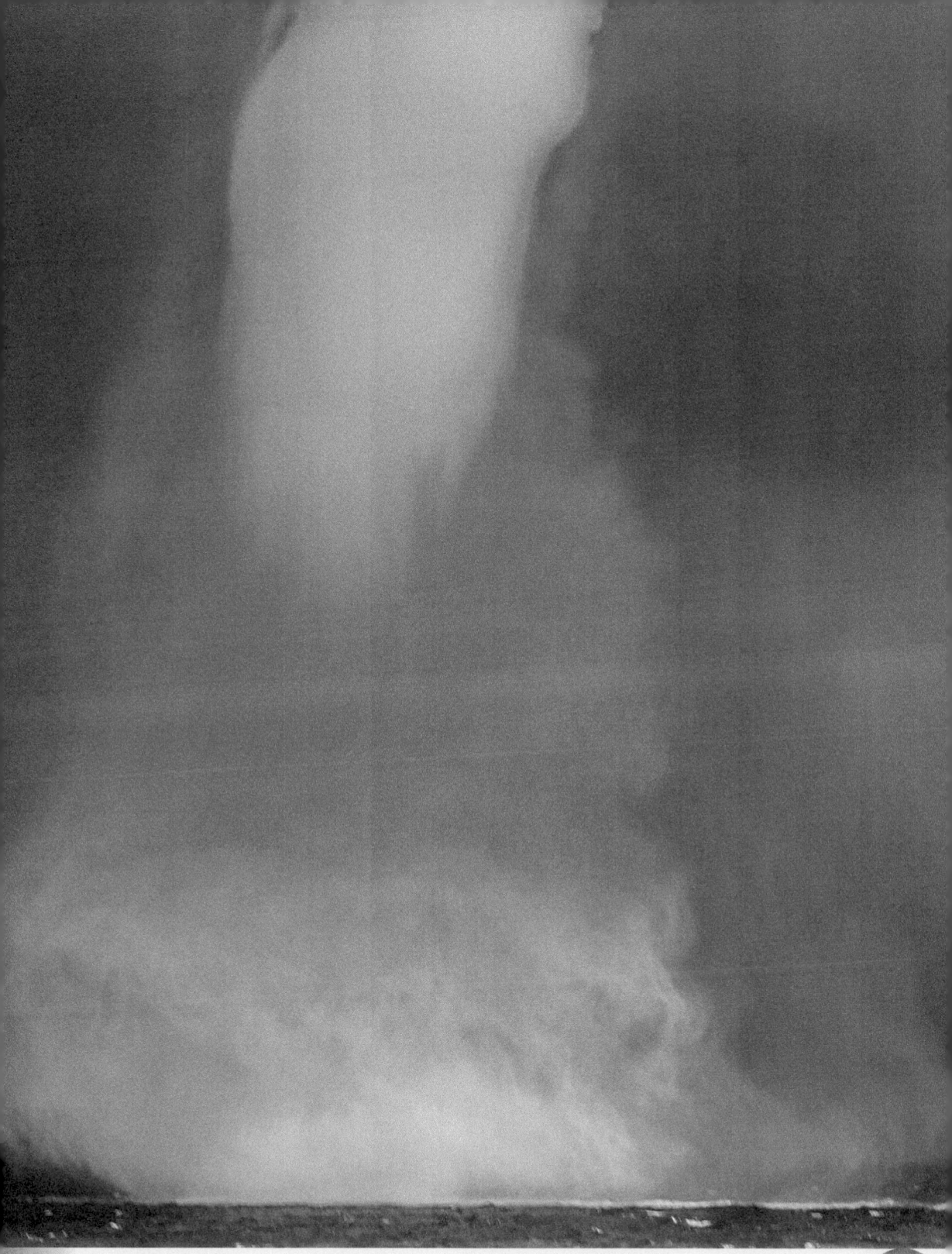

**hurricane**—a very large storm with high winds and rain that forms over an ocean

When a **tornado warning** sounds, head for the nearest basement or storm shelter. Get under a stairwell or stay in a hallway. Most of all, keep away from windows. Tornadoes are nature's fiercest storms. Knowing where to go will help keep you safe from their awesome power.

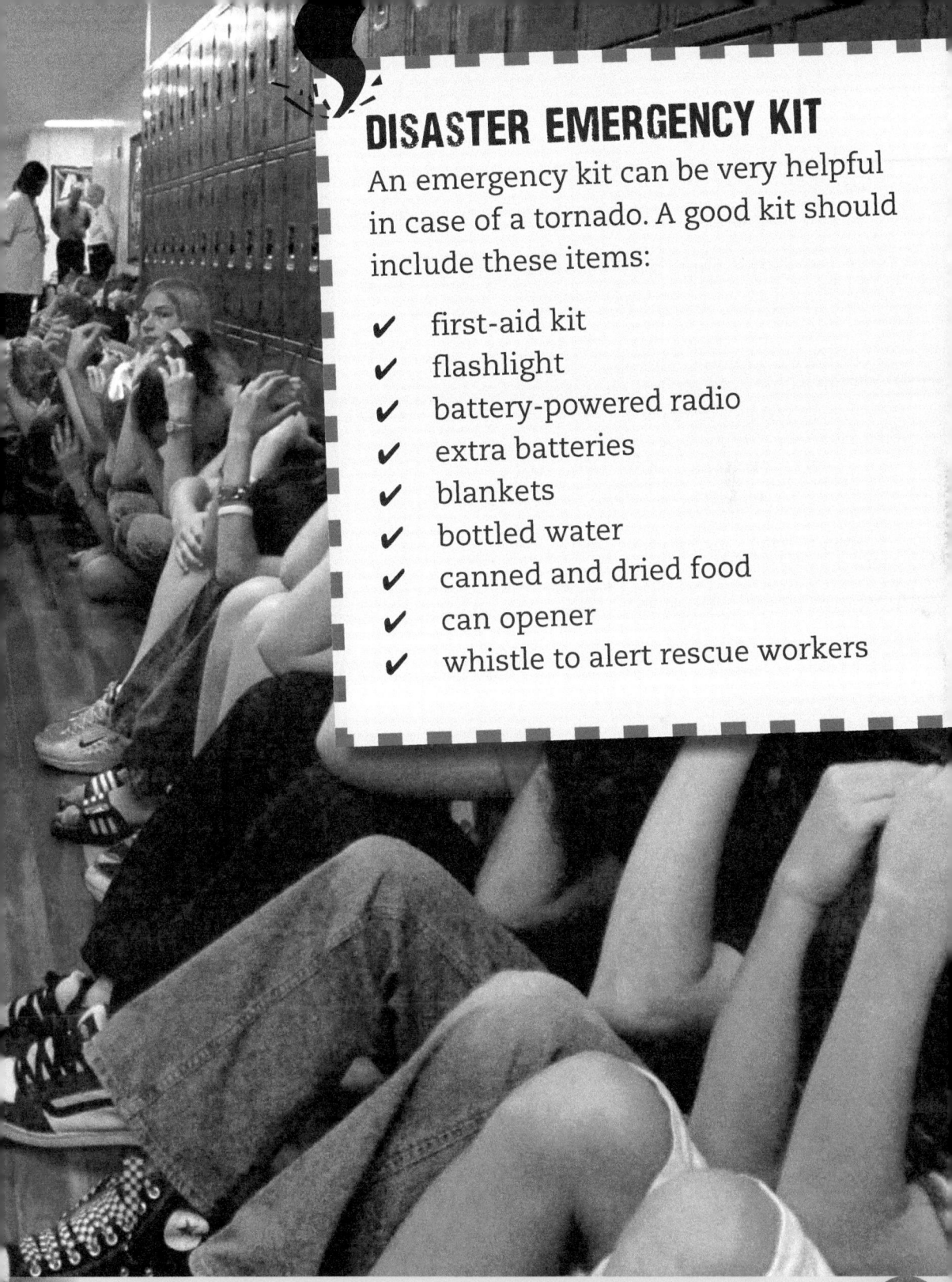

## DISASTER EMERGENCY KIT

An emergency kit can be very helpful in case of a tornado. A good kit should include these items:

- ✔ first-aid kit
- ✔ flashlight
- ✔ battery-powered radio
- ✔ extra batteries
- ✔ blankets
- ✔ bottled water
- ✔ canned and dried food
- ✔ can opener
- ✔ whistle to alert rescue workers

**tornado warning**—an alert issued when a tornado has been seen or is expected soon

# GLOSSARY

**cyclone** (SY-klohn)—a fast spinning column of air

**debris** (duh-BREE)—the scattered pieces of something that has been broken or destroyed

**hail** (HAYL)—balls of ice that fall during a thunderstorm

**humid** (HYOO-mid)—damp and moist

**hurricane** (HUR-uh-kane)—a very large storm with high winds and rain that forms over an ocean

**outbreak** (OUT-brake)—a large number of events that occur in a certain area

**tornado warning** (tor-NAY-doh WOR-ning)—an alert issued when a tornado has been seen or is expected soon

# READ MORE

**Challoner, Jack.** *Eyewitness Hurricane & Tornado*. DK Eyewitness. New York: DK Publishing, 2014.

**Garbe, Suzanne.** *Threatening Skies: History's Most Dangerous Weather*. Dangerous History. North Mankato, Minn.: Capstone Press, 2014.

**Rustad, Martha E. H.** *Tornadoes: Be Aware and Prepare*. Weather Aware. North Mankato, Minn.: Capstone Press, 2015.

# INTERNET SITES

Facthound offers a safe, fun way to find Internet sites related to this book. All of the sites on Facthound have been researched by our staff.

Here's all you do:
Visit *www.facthound.com*
Type in this code: 9781515717881

# CRITICAL THINKING USING THE COMMON CORE

1. Tornadoes often kill people and cause huge amounts of damage. Which tornado was the deadliest in history? Which one was the costliest? (Key Ideas and Details)
2. Explain what you should do if you hear a siren signaling a tornado warning. (Craft and Structure)
3. Look at the chart on pages 4–5. What are the wind speeds for each category of tornado on the EF scale? (Integration of Knowledge and Ideas)

# INDEX


Brisbane, Australia, 23
Bucca, Australia, 23
casualties, 6, 8, 11, 12, 15, 18, 21
damage costs, 8, 11, 15, 19
Dhaka, Bangladesh, 12
emergency kits, 29
Enhanced Fujita (EF) Scale, 4–5
hail, 23
Hallam, Nebraska, 24, 25
homeless victims, 13, 21
Hurricane Ivan, 26
International Tornado Intensity Scale, 17
Joplin, Missouri, 15
Norfolk county, Great Britain, 16
Oklahoma City, Oklahoma, 8, 9
Regina, Canada, 21
staying safe, 28
Topeka, Kansas, 18, 19
tornadoes
  nicknames of, 7
  outbreaks of, 10, 16, 26
  records of, 6, 9, 10, 12, 15, 16, 23, 24, 26
  warnings, 28
  wind speeds of, 5, 9, 23